travelogue
of the bereaved

poems

by
charles c. smith

We acknowledge the support of the Canada Council for the Arts for our publishing program. We also acknowledge support from the Government of Ontario through the Ontario Arts Council.

We acknowledge the financial support of the Government of Canada through the Canada Book Fund for our publishing activities.

ONTARIO ARTS COUNCIL
CONSEIL DES ARTS DE L'ONTARIO
an Ontario government agency
un organisme du gouvernement de l'Ontario
Canada Council for the Arts
Conseil des arts du Canada
Canada

Cover art: *Shelter 3 - 2011,* by Jerome Havre
Cover design by Peggy Stockdale

Library and Archives Canada Cataloguing in Publication

smith, charles c., 1953-, author
Travelogue of the bereaved : poems / by charles c. smith.

ISBN 978-1-927494-34-9 (pbk.)

I. Title.

PS8637.M5595T73 2014 C811'.6 C2014-902077-5

Printed and bound in Canada by Coach House Printing

TSAR Publications
P. O. Box 6996, Station A
Toronto, Ontario M5W 1X7
Canada
www.tsarbooks.com

The project for black Canadian artists and critics is to articulate a grammar of black that is located within Canada's various regions, both urban and rural. The invention of a grammar for black in Canada that is aware of historical narrative and plays with that narrative is crucial in the struggle against erasure . . . The articulation of a grammar for black, and ensuing contestations over it, is what will continue to imbibe the vital cultures of black Canadians with a continued dynamism . . . A grammar for black will cement blackness to the nation and reconfigure the nation for the better.

—RINALDO WALCOTT, in *Black Like Who?*

Contents

lettin' it all hang out

drums and piano

make me wanna holla'

1st voice

for oliver lejeune and matthieu dacosta

did anyone ever stop
to measure the distance you were
from where you were born?

one without origin traveling words
across portugal and spain netherlands and france—

the other caught up in madagascar
herded on ranges boarded on boats—

how strange it must have been
to be drawn away by those who were far from home
and who took you as if thru irons and coals

then carried you over an ocean
to service them in a continent of blood—

no need to spell out the rewards—
they fed clothed and kept you
as if they did not want you to be alone—

and you stayed close
as if you could never be without them—

a boy and a man servant and guide
reliably noteworthy of your place—

they made you what you were—
you replied in kind

gave them bedclothes   rendered mi'kmaq
opened borders   for cleanliness and trade—

and letting them   reach beyond you
you dug into the bowels   of their suspicions

like the song of a bird   coming from inside a cloud
each moment   you walked into a room

and you knew   who you were
when they spoke to you   with words

of a very recognizable   order—

new france

"local records reveal   3,604 separate slaves
by 1759   . . . 1,132 negroes"

55.2%   in or near montreal
caged in the open   barring escape

hardly any near mines   fields

scattered in the hills
or close to   a river or lake—

22.8% at work   across the land
digging up earth   setting down farm houses and towns—

life expectancy   "panis" 17.5 years
blacks a little longer   25.2

only to disadvantage   those who pay
the funeral expense—

1,509 owners   for 962 different families
181 english   ¼ (1,068) belonging to merchants
gentry governors   notaries doctors military and the church—

most managing 2-3   at a time—

"84 half-breeds   19 mulattos"
who in turn married   and in turn
bled into quad—   and octoroon whiteness—

573 children without adequate record
59.5% born away from marriage

97 "panis" children bastards
32.1% the suspect dark child—

death by thirty

for marie joseph angelique and phyllis wheatly

so you were both   gone
by then   stretched into distances
between who   you really were
and what   you wore
when your lungs went cold   and you could not breathe
and the sound of your own   eyes shutting
invited   the curved limits of night—

how did this happen?   one
compelled by violence   the flame
that took down a city
                                         the other
cursed with freedom   and a way
with words—
                                          one
confessing innocence   over and over
until tortured
                        the other
abandoned by poetry   and the arms of a man—

each of you went   a blaze
in your eyes   extinguishing all light

purse-less   with nothing to spend to end your suffering—

the english east coast

a "negro servant . . . orange . . .   mentioned in a will" 1752
j. mauger esquire   put several up for sale

1759 m. salter   commissioned his wife to buy him a boy
while commenting   he took " . . . the cat or stick"

to one black body   every day—

1760 liverpool   "a boy and a girl . . . 11 years old . . .
(and) . . . choice cherry brandy"—

1767 new glasgow   and the "rascal negro" who
"cannot be flattered or drove   to do one-fourth a man's work"—

1768   2,217 bodies valued at L77,795 sterling
imported into the caribbean america newfoundland—

1769 halifax auction on the beach
"two hogsheads of rum three of sugar and two well-grown negro girls"—

1770 bridgetown amherst onslaw cornwallis
with 5-17   at mount denson alone

and at camden and edwardsburgh   in deed to
p. russell w. jarvis j. and r. isaac gray   p. robinson
m. elliot j. brant and w. davis   who arrived

from north carolina   with a grandfather clock
peach stones carpet   and "several faithful slaves"—

capt. a. barclay   and his company of 55
held 57   for 4 private estates—

c.o. brueff 15 s. shakespeare j. and a. robertson
all from the u.s. each with 20″

and in fredericton where "distinguished virginia
and maryland loyalist" b.robinson resided

"son of a speaker of the house of burgesses of virginia . . .
member first council new brunswick"—

along with i.allen and lieutenant-governor e.fanning
former supreme court judges for north carolina and new jersey—

1784 port roseway muster records 1,269—

assuming the costs

millwrights blacksmiths carpenters caregivers sawyers caulkers printers
carrying children carving fences shoeing horses paving roads—

1743 women at 800 livres and in 1749 one went for 1000
1748 and 1751 negro men at 4—500
1757 "a boy in his prime . . . 1,192"

another late 1770s at L50 in truro
a man and a horse in 1780s at L40 in one deal—

in new france the usual fare 20 to L60—

a woman purchased in 1778 for L50 then sold
the following year with cloth and linen—

sarah at L65 and let go for L36 and in 1789
sold twice for 36 and L40—

1785, 1801 and 1832 (even tho illegal) those brought in
from elsewhere 43—L60

(except 1790s in lower canada 25—L100
and once for 213)

millwrights blacksmiths carpenters caregivers sawyers caulkers printers

treaties and promises

> to every negro who shall desert the rebel standard, full security to follow within these lines, any occupation which he shall think proper
>
> —*Philipsburg Proclamation*, 1779

and for this   you traveled so far
held a rifle   watched others die as you lay

face down   in the cold rain
of some territory   in northern pennsylvania—

for this   dream of a promise
for land   you got up and left

with the last   bullet
followed   white loyalists

and carried your wives   and children
across a long vague border   into freedom

then you woke   in such desolate places
(birchtown annapolis halifax fredericton isle st. jean)

slicing winds and damp   cut off from commerce and wealth
kept in the sweat   of a hatred

even tho   you were offered more
before bullets   fell into disuse

and announced   the "new
beginning"   south of the border
the birth of states   and a regime built by slaves—

this is what you left   when you landed
and you could not   tell the difference—

the same bodies   worked fields
houses hand trades   horses and mules

cleaning kitchens   birthing babies
shadowing other children   into their adult years

and seemingly   always for nothing—
each attempt   barely keeping off

bare cupboards   and cold stoves—

birchtown in flames

just outside shelbourne   july 1784
an "extraordinary mob   or riot"

unemployed disbanded soldiers   with guns
found their way   to the other side

drowning churches and houses   with torches
herding men and women   children and dogs

and leaving some   sucking stones—
the skies full of clouds   smoke and stars

caves became sepulchres   without light
and blood ran into roots   like a downpour

so that the wooded roads   rushed red
between   these two towns

one full of transactions   like a crescent
moon bartering   with night

the other caught up   like a snake in a garter
all of its venom   squeezed out at the teeth

one built on white lace   foodstuffs and rum
anchoring boats   from the stretches of an early empire

the other veiled in emptiness   taking each day
like a prayer   and trading all they had

both slammed hammers   into this port city
while others   gambled the differences

between those who worked   and what they were paid
by the official surveyor   who too faced weapons that were
suddenly unconcealed

until the army   sat in a warship in the harbour
and birchtown   lay cindered in an open field

then the tally   in stock and bodies
all assets liabilities fatalities   the tabulations seemingly endless

claims and counters in courtrooms   the early jurisprudence of this state—
and as always   after recording property and labour

there was no time given   for other stories

brittain murray

1786

and so you found the cost
was all you had to make due
and it took everything out of you

these forests of discomfort
these cold and seemingly permanent rules
these consistent indignities

you imagined them fresh out of memory
where they found their place

in the noise of those gathered in the early light
for a public display

when you woke to men holding your biceps and wrists
and dragging you out of a prison cell into daylight—

their abrupt and sudden surge guiding your arms
your hips and thighs then quickened into sludge
your spine sprung out like a frog—

all in the flash of a command
they held on to you
and in this form of judgment made you history—

so how could you manage to contain it? how
could your bulky black frame glide as if on wings?

clearly something was going very badly
and you were caught up in it—

your toes in the grip of mid-air
body suspended upon a dangling line

the laws of the day held you in contempt
so rendered you lifeless beneath a gibbet of wood—

what could you say in return?

you came so completely into this
taking each breath like a life knotted with boundaries

so much so that it was almost
as if you held your own head in your hands

and twisted it left and right
until it broke—

josiah cutten

1789

> (his) crime is so much more atrocious and alarming to society as it is committed by night when the world is at repose . . . and (he) resembled animals that go prowling about in the night for their prey

quite the honour   you received—
the first to be legally hanged   in upper canada—

before that   you were
in and out of irons   across massachusetts michigan quebec

poorly clothed   in the grimace of ice and snow
callouses blisters warts   covering your slim body—

once freed   you were charged with break and enter
for something as simple   as furs and rum—

then behind bars   you were
sold again   before being convicted

only to leave your new master   with all your costs
since the judge   sentenced you

to be strung up off the ground   with your neck
stuck at the end   of a thick tight rope

at the gallows   in sandwich ontario—

other ways

1791 one dropped
trying to make his way into a dance

1792 justice william dummer powell
sentences another to hang for burglary

1795 a seventeen-year-old
given the same sentence by a jury—

w jarvis tries two of his own
for "stealing gold and silver"—

jupiter property of the russels
tied up all day in a storage barn—

in bath a tree used to secure a beating
becomes a local landmark—

in annapolis one gone from whipping
the splits in his body spilling screams—

felled with a hammer in windsor nova scotia
while in truro a hole cut in the ear

fit with a whiplash dragged one down the street—

and w brown the printer who paid five shillings
has the executioner whip his slave boy joe

in a market place in quebec—

difficult property

how the words were all of you
each letter spelling assumptions
linked to auction price fixed/negotiable
age expectancy of service
demeanor sometimes noted only to set
rest to rumour of ill-will negligence or hostility

> *february 19, 1806, to be sold: a black woman named peggy, aged forty, and a black boy, her son, named jupiter, aged fifteen . . . the woman is a tolerable cook and washerwoman, and perfectly understands making soap and candles. the boy is tall and strong for his age, and has been employed in the country business, but brought up principally as a house servant. they are each . . . servants for life . . .*

and so you were quilled mid-market
an entry between bidders and the curious
eyeing each side of a sale

amidst cattle wood and housewares
quilts and tools corn barley and hay
rum and sugar by the "hogshead"

earthenware pottery sometimes even perfume—

> *my slave peggy, whom you were so good to promise to assist getting rid of, has remained in prison ever since you left this (in expectation of your sending for her) at an expense of above ten pounds halifax, which i was obliged to pay to...release her*

in such a way
the unimaginable set with words
wrung from what seemed another language
—full of signatures and possessives—

over bodies bound in homes and fields
as if in boxes locked with warnings—

what began as a walk off a platform
down make-shift steps to a dirt road
partially fenced along a narrow street

soon stretched past wooden storefronts
painted framed two storeys and standing
in that place where small town borders fade—

a small parade into expectations
and troubled into service like a carousal
that fit every corner of their lives
like a key—

> *i shall therefore be glad that you would either take her away immediately, or return to me the bill of sale . . . for tho i have received no money from you for her, my property in her is gone . . . and i cannot consequently give a valid title to any other than who may be inclined to take her off my hands . . .*

over and over   dull scenes in small squares
voices price bodies   to the last bid

and they stand there   eyes at skies
as if at longing—

between their hips   their swagger
lost at the knees   bent in the bled wind

only to enter into   transaction
a receipt and bill of sale   written as debit/credit
of some private tethering   over estates

any special instruction spoken openly

bonds non-negotiable   no sale final
without inspection   and references
(when available)   especially
for those with child—

> *. . . a gentleman going to england has for sale a negro wench, with her child . . . she understands thoroughly every kind of housework, particularly washing and cookery. and a stout negro boy 13 years old. also a good horse, cariole and harness . . .*

> *. . . for sale, a negro slave, 18 years of age, stout and healthy, has had the smallpox and is capable of service either in the house or out of doors . . .*

> *. . . for sale, negro man and woman, property of mrs. widow clement. they have been bred to the work of the farm; will be sold on highly advantageous terms for cash or lands . . .*

> *. . . wanted to purchase, a negro girl from seven to twelve years age of good disposition. for full particulars, apply to . . .*

purchased posted and sold
stuck in the ink of property

each gesture recoiling in dream
what you were and what it might mean
to be on your own in another direction

at the edges of villages and towns
so many hours through lakes and fields
south emptying every trace or trail

imagined in such a simple horror
running out of blindness without a destination

just some vague border escape thru water
rock and bush with breath a cloud of stars
and coyotes clearing the distance
beneath a thimble moon—

> *quebec gazette, july 29, 1769*
> *joseph negrie, . . . 22 . . . brown complexion, slim . . . 5 feet 3 inches . . . small legs, speaks french and english tolerably well, ran away . . . between 7th and the 8th instant . . . the public is desired not to employ the said negrie, and all captains of vessals who may take him on board are forewarned from carrying him out of the province, as they will be pursued to the utmost rigour of the law . . .*

no trust or rest in caves
in marshlands that led to
hollowed-out trunks of trees

no walking alone
into the agony of surrender

with eyes open you slept
and woke with stealth to find
eggs apples peaches greens

gambling in farm yards
with watchdogs and shotguns
"peppering" double trails—

then to hear of posters promising reward—

> *in february 1798, charlotte ran out on her mistress. in the absence of any recorded explanation of her motives, we are left to wonder what could have impelled a slave, who had stuck by the cook family through more than twenty years, to jump ship in the depths of a montreal winter? it had to have been more than a whim. fear for her own safety? if cook had grown abusive and beat her, this might have given charlotte reason to run for cover, but there is not the slightest hint that this was the case. separation from a loved one? this is a possibility. the threat of imminent sale? this seems like the probable cause . . .*

so you breathed into this uncertainty
always expecting confrontation

that moment when you would be
stripped of everything

and led back
through spaces you had passed
moving darkness to darkness

to find a place you knew nothing of
and to linger like some phantom
in a netherworld of endless need

deafened by sounds that stretched your memory
into a rare disease—

and distracted you
from wondering how much more
you could take before falling

broken and done
in some other land pressed without shadows

without vials of wisdom set in the bloodless spleen

across centuries

for chloe cooley

no ordinary walk to the river   you were held
by three men   tied and tossed into a boat

then led across darkness   into new york

and the sounds you made   enveloped the night
like light   surrounding eclipsed clouds—

a woman   pushing lines thru your hue
you made others   hear across centuries

what was howled   in the boats' bellies
and deep inside the hard white crests   of cold atlantic waves—

from the mouth   of a free man who heard you
you caught   another's ears

and he started to fill   the official record
with the swelling pain of language   rationality and reason

and drinks   before and after debate
amongst men   who owned several slaves—

meanwhile
you had to struggle   just to breathe

and no one stopped   your sale
or kept you   from crossing over water into night

nor did any   hold your captors
or tear up   the legal contract and receipt—

you were gone without obstruction
save your own voice in the still night air

and the story of dominion you challenged

your body pressed into the bow of a boat
then thrown across borders

to care for a house and field—

free at last

between 1798 and 1833

"the principles of the british constitution do not admit of that slavery which christianity condemns. the moment i assume the government of upper canada under no modification will i assent to a law that discriminates by dishonest policy between natives of africa, america or europe."

—LT. GOVERNOR SIMCOE

this is what they wanted us to say
that we found our way into heaven well-dressed

wore words so openly given
like fine clothes drawn on a sheet of paper

signed by the governor-general of upper canada
who says who we are

and even more those to be paid
if ever any of us were let go

thru that bleak door opened into night
like some river prolonged into emptiness—

nothing was left when we walked
neither work food nor land

house nor horse
only the tattered garments of belief

we would wear to disguise
this new-found equality

bound up   with the leisure of those
who set our release   into the future

as if we were to be   pleased each moment
our lives   were given over once again

to bondage   and the small hope our children
will have   what we've dreamed

and not be left   without dreaming—

making it to st. catherines

for william and delia cornish

you turned her over   each day
six times   to keep her warm and breathing

otherwise   she could not move
several months   inside this bed—

the passage   too cold and fatiguing
over sharp stones   cold rivers

thru towns   and people
exchanging bodies   for reward—

her feet iced   into bruises and bone
you tend   to her now

even tho you   just sat up
two days   before her arrival

and this the coldest   of winters

your own escape   treacherous
you hold her   in your arms

your every gesture   looking to comfort
those you knew   lost in the fields—

a calling

they say   harriet and john
plotted together   recruited in st. catherines

any   willing to return their anger
in the cause of freedom   rifles loaded

at the gate   of harper's ferry

maryann shadd

long before other women
you ran a newspaper started schools
let your voice ripple across the 49th and 51st line

neither home here or south of the border
staggered by brandings and whiplash
struck by bondsmen and shackles

at words with churches and abolitionists
who wanted nothing more than separate spaces
to house black bodies on their own

(in elgin dawn buxton winchester sandwich
haiti jamaica and sierra leone)

you used a man's name in print
but not amongst suffragettes
who had other ways to keep their distance

yet with both you cut a syntax
fierce and uncensored
and what those children you taught
learned became the call to all you left
across southern fields and eastern coasts
and within mid-western farms—

this was the space you balanced
and it was all that mattered
what your body told you
because of breasts buttocks blackness

what your words spelled inside the *provincial freeman*
when you crossed these lines
with everything you ever held precious
riding like lightning through this northern air

you were driven then across boundaries
in ways only a few could understand
so built your work like a well out of the earth

in chatham and windsor where you set down
into an endless resistance—

john brown in upper canada

i
imagine an average-sized white man
wild greying hair sharp green eyes

intent on only one thing "insurrection"
he spent months in chatham and st. catherines with black men

wanting return to anything that would take them from winter
and let them have once again the place where they once belonged

and where the surface of suffering was
already beyond the usual brutal death—

he called moses "general" a rank higher than his own
this woman who found slaves homes in exile

and trespassed regularly across the wastes and darkness
cold waters sharp cutting grass thistle and thorns

he saw in her the guts of several men
sought her counsel and company

recognized a spirit heated as his own

ii
fire in each vein urgency igniting breath
they saw their call to arms crawl into beds
in the deep south and treacherous north

into fields where sweat glistened like glass beads
on bodies buried under an unrelenting sun—

this was the agony   he wanted lanced
by any means necessary   by his stock of weapons

his grip on a trigger   danger covered the field
in this seemingly blind   and reckless suicide

iii

but this is where he wanted to be
on foot in a barrack shoving men into uniform
bullets into smoke teasing death

his every breath held one ambition
the earth trembling under horses' hooves
skies flashing like hyperboles

chatham and st. catherines were simply spaces
to forecast what was never to come
the dream he had in the middle of the night
his sheets sweated with anxiety—

but what else did he know?   what
other ways had he considered?

with soldiers trembling in such
random and absolute violence
he never saw his last days
and his sons gone before him

their hearts split like whispers
when lee stampeded with cannon
horses and men spitting light
out of the urinals of day

iv

so how does one live after this? what words

can settle such debt ensuring all regrets
—either his or those under his command—
are not left lingering in a shroud?

who will remember the day he disappeared
like a fox into his own miscalculation
and sat in a prison cell awaiting the certain
outcome of a trial for treason?

what happens with this story
of risk and abandon?
                                        of a white man
driven to end the seemingly endless
suffering of those made to bow
to the cleaned and pressed

white coats of privilege?—

visions

once dined on the grass at woodmere
looking on as the queen of england passed—

a grand carriage her portly dress trimmed
with precious stones silk and lace—

she was sunlight her glow
spreading out over florid surroundings

hard to believe she did not blind her escort—

he sat calm touching her hand so full of empire
so full her thoughts wet on her lips—

perhaps she thinks of germany
its brutish peoples waking into nation

or yet she considers hot rum from the islands
distilled by hands as fevered as their skin—

she lifts a flask
sips once then again her smile

floating like a wafer down dull streets full of commoners
her carriage winds its way into the west wall of the city

where children throw rose petals under wheels
then run and gasp and smile as if they had seen heaven—

george

for the pullman porters
from toronto and montreal

. . . so you ran the rails
made everyone's stay worthwhile

serving politeness
with that imitation southern smile—

you walked train cars
in and out of cabins kitchens baths

feeding children shining shoes—
turning down covers and sheets

you put it all together
the way you would a song in the air

half sung in the chorus like a field of smoke
over charred bodies swinging in trees—

a tray full of drinks decks of cards
patrons hurling insults and jeers

all day every day for seven days
white men in your face
and staying clear of white women's eyes—

you went across two countries
shirt pressed in respectful silence
as if you were servicing a sacred child

you felt you owed your life to
and that the words that formed in your cheeks
to tell anyone about this

could only come out as they did
without anger—

but with the run of a cut tongue
sliding down your cheeks like rain—

as if there were no charges

in susanna moody we read
how a man on his wedding night

is dragged across rails into death—

then there is the trail of cars
with hooded men ("except the one driving")

and the tall cross they left
burning in oakville's downtown—

thirty years later
the father of a bride-to-be
pays for a hit in hamilton—

and what were each of them charged?

one who escaped public record
and lives in the shadow of another's story?

others with the sheriff accepting
their "gentlemanly disposition"

or the argument in court
evading conviction?

or was it simply the particular intolerances
in a city becoming full of its differences

in a nation awash in its wish to disown its past?

it meant very little to drag a black body
out of his house on his wedding night
and into the stark light of evening—

it meant even less to burn his house down
after those released from charges

forcibly separated him from his future bride—

and then to watch all of this find
a parent out to protect his bloodline—

one run into another realm
the other with an escort of 75

and the man who took the future bride's hands
and led her to a car to bring her "home"—

much like the other
who barricaded his daughter with heredity—

one with a five-month
the other with a five-year sentence

and then the first seemingly unknown—

viola desmond in doubt

those feet get tired   it happened
early evening   just after you left your car—

dressed   in a fine wool hat
pressed   black coat

collar turned up in the evening dampness

you walked   past the hotel
to a local theatre

paid full fare   went down the main floor
searching   for a good seat

'til the police   took you out
for not paying   a one cent tax—

your shoe   falling in the aisle

it seemed   to strike you
like a cut   stone

a torn curve   in the memory
when you were   hauled

onto the street   a sack of fur—

and then spent your night   behind bars

where neither you   nor your words
could be   contained—

so you were released
into custody to serve

beyond what they could make
through a quick conviction—

and this put you on call
across courtrooms and headlines

each instance making you wish
you could only just crawl away

into some more silent humiliation—

nigger rock

and some of those who arrived as slaves
have disappeared into their names

so what wonder that this could be its name

a graveyard marked with a large black rock
last and only home for such bodies in quebec—

gathered in the very earth they wrestled
centuries later their lives found surface

thru memories broken in the public gaze
they were suddenly present
hands that bent shovels and ploughs

finding words eyes and ears
asking what could ever be an appropriate measure
to remember any of this?

or a reasonable expectation to recast
the days they tilled light and dark

their absence planted in memory—
not a fool on the hill but a nigger on the rock

over time smoothing darkness off faces
marrying shadow into archives

all evidence of who they were
diminished by their own hands—

lettin′ it all hang out

marlon neal

1974-1990

each day you walked on an asphalt sea
and faced an horizon of concrete—

your young mind filled with so many things
bicycles and ice cream soccer and basketball
and dreams of sun mounting waters
that do not warm the coldness of these cold borders—

but what did you do to know of nights whose eyes
were bright spots lunging into the face?

why were you in such a conspicuous position
when that white and blue car blocked your path
and pushed you into a corner like a slug?

what did you learn from the heart of this
and the moments when your sad anger
was drowned by a warning call and gunfire?

what could you have forecast that would have
been a better description—

some back alley of a bad dream in which you die?

and you can only watch yourself
a sack of flesh sinking into concrete—

the heat of things

you wake out of darkness into night
a gun in the bedside table drawer—

you have priorities like everyone else—
getting out of this house alive—

you plan on it like an accountant forecasting stocks
(investment in sunlight)—

so you hide inside windows and doors
behind pots and pans and old mouse traps

and guard the fire escape like steps to a temple
since the day you found a dead dog in the grass

a prostitute fallen on her sleeves
veins rolled up into needles

and children playing in the poorly paved parking lot
running out of the way of police cars—

and with what the next hour will bring always uncertain
you head into sunset

imagining escape
arms spread like wings of a heron fading into the east—

bullet proof

for wade lawson

because you were somewhere "you shouldn't have been"
because your hands on the steering wheel were so tight
your knuckles thinned into lighter hues

because it was night and you had been told this would happen
and that you would sit seemingly endlessly on the edge of rage
as if you hit on something sharp and always in your jeans

because you were so thoroughly unprepared
to be for this moment surrounded and almost invisible

because you changed lanes and signalled for a turn
at the street light and into the presence of a police cruiser

because everything done by someone like you is seen as an invasion

because the distance between your car and the one in front of you
was supposedly abrupt when you supposedly exhibited
a dangerous handling of a dangerous vehicle

because it seemed you had something to hide
and looked and moved about furtively

because your window seemed to be open on a cool night
and it seemed smoke was coming out in streams

because there seemed to be someone else in your car
looking about as you did over and over again
hiding under his hat and fading into his seat

because you began to sweat when you saw
the lights of the police car "inexplicably" behind you

because you like so many others drove down streets
looking for fun with your windows open music blaring
looking for a friend to ride "shotgun" across suburban streets

because on this spring night with your hair picked out
you were simply wanting to show off your "new ride"

because no officer was down but you were out
and your mother harrowed in disbelief wore headlines
to the room where you lay breathless
awaiting the coroner and the official report—

the special investigation unit standing like altar boys
silently watching from the aisle—

another casualty

and what does it mean   to be in prison?
each day you ask yourself   sitting at home

working alone   staring
at a wall   of north african masks

(ghana burkino faso nigeria tanzania)—

over a cup of tea   you search out
this confinement   and how a group of bureaucrats

put you   in this place
when they   decided to get rid of you

one way or another   like some old world soviet spy—

now you sit at a pile of papers   preparing another report
for those   who really don't give a damn

about what you pulled out   in the ugliness of places
where the cut eyes of children   bled behind prison bars

tributaries to ancestors   whose bones
were bleached   on battlefields—

so many spirits
buried beneath huge stones   in closed caves

beneath the gaze of soldiers   razing
empires   like so much seed—

somehow they ignored   the crimes they committed
like mobsters who simply wanted   to go home—

it was as if they knew
it was only always a breath away   from a turn
in the back of a police cruiser   where you
would see your own   dark skin in the rearview

along with fields   of loss and betrayal
lies and the suddenness   of endings
like what   was at your door when you were thrown
to the floor   and you knew what your sentence was

and why it was so real—

sophia cook

so you proved everyone wrong
wearing a skirt instead of trousers
and in one breath making clear a connection
you probably never thought of—

your body pressed into headlines
along with albert buddy wade
marlon and so many others

you didn't need to have your hair
pulled out or dragged before judges
to feel the humiliation of being

brought down for nothing
in the middle of a street
in the middle of the night
surrounded by uniforms

night sticks handcuffed
wrists and faces pressed
into the glass of a police cruiser

when you were shot in the leg
for sitting on the passenger side
of a suspect car—

what the press says

they tell us we are not fathers
that we drop our seed like nameless parasites

lounging in shadows
past moonlit stars and clouds—

they complain we were not schooled
in the cool arts of deceit

and so never had any intent
on anything anyone anytime anyplace—

we only let our tongues hang out in lies
and allow others to tell how we live this "irresponsible abandon"

unaccountable dangerous seemingly only wanting to fly

even tho we hear our mothers' hearts carrying
the graves of their loved ones downed in senseless attacks—

the streets we seem to have chosen assume a destiny

all else is a matter of what the morning brings
measuring the chance each moment we move

obliged by a possible profitable momentary enterprise—

we go where we go to hell with others
no one knows what and how we live or why—

our breath only useful for its value in newspapers

it is alright then to point out how early we all seem to die
and by what means by what street corner by whose hand—

we are given no right to complain so frivolous our needs
even tho it is our bones placed against what matters in your eyes

as you dream you were at holiday in the caribbean
where young and old cracked black hands serve

themselves as offerings—

blues and reggae

dark blue night rises over the sparkling cn tower
surrounds it in a seemingly impenetrable ocean mist

a pale half-moon shadows a stretch of condominiums
windows flicker white lights like jewellers flashing gems

across the street a tall man walks a golden retriever
a small boy lunges by on a yellow and blue skateboard

a mother pulls a stroller up to the curb and rocks
her child who has fallen asleep

cars glide by slowly before fading into the east
a siren breaks the deafening silence

after a skidding of wheels and crackling fire
two black youth swim in blood

and their mothers gather around them
on the pavement outside an apartment building

hands wringing useless dim lit summer air
they howl under blinking stars like hungry wolves

going the distance

onions frying   a smell in the air
sharp and pungent   cold meat put down
carefully   as if the last touch of collage
a red piece   primitive rawness—

all else silence—
neither you   nor the woman cooking
spoke   'til knife and fork were idle
a ritual   that didn't need words
every wednesday   the months of winter
when arena crowds   were driven
into an alcoholic   frenzy
fists popping   greased brows
blood spurting   onto a rawhide canvas
the instant "hurrahs"   overwhelm a clanging
bell   as a man in a short-sleeved shirt
lifted a tall boy's body   fragile as a thin reed
up from a final count—

then your hands   twin flags waving
adrenalin   fever-pitched
one week later   the sequence repeated
you walked into those days   head high
as a gamecock   trembling for connection
to those you knew   and didn't know—

something other   than a piece of cold meat
slapped down   into the sizzling blue
flames of an arena—

drive by

listening to louis armstrong blow
his strange arc of blues
out into the new orleans streets of 1920

i think of those in toronto
gunned down outside their homes
bullets squealing like saxophones

rounding out the reeds
of this music of suffering—

i think of their last words
begging mercy like shrill clarinets
or accompanying like a pianist

who will not do a solo this night
when the trumpet is a lone gun
hot on a mission

to press into memory
the tunes he can play—

i think of their half-limp swagger
their pants half-down thin sapphire legs

their silver bracelets and chains
dangling in the cool breeze
of a rhythm section

that has just turned hot
as blood rolls in the street
along the sides of a chalk-marked figure

face down against black asphalt
below a phosphorescent sky
choked with indifference—

with these dull marks
signing the night "a la nelly
st. louis style"   i hear satchmo's trumpet

beside the keys of "fatha" hines
then think   whom these cools
have left   in agony

relatives friends lovers children
their spontaneity   like gunfire
a bursting polyphony   from the open window
of a speeding car—

escape

wind flies into startled faces   down long
wide avenues   masked in black asphalt
and faded white street lines   where empty

street cars ride out   the middle of the night
dim secrets   of distant violent lives—

you sat in the back   looking out the plate glass
rain-splotched window behind you   a "young gun"

with a cool lip   two gold necklaces flashing
diamond studded pierced ears   and chains   around
your thin waist   like a child ready to walk a faithful dog—

with your blue-green toque   warming a baseball cap
and black headphones   wagging like ears

you ran   out of a night club
whose flashing neon lights   burst

into gunfire   in the ignited room
where you crawled   like an infant in a broken playpen

off the emptying   dance floor
past the bar stools   filled with muscle-toned dealers

flamboyant pimps   their gold and platinum
teeth   flashing madness in the near perfect dark—

onlookers   moving away
from the front doors   steamed windows
and cracked   black and grey sidewalks

they greeted you as bodies tumbled over
into gutters like punch-drunk boxers staggering
into daylight outside a moving ring—

you left them at curbside and found
an opening down an alley that led
to a streetcar's headlights

gleaming on empty sidewalks like the eyes
of some wild animal stalking a kill—

then you jumped thru opened red doors
and moved slowly past the tired
bearded face of a young white man

working a second shift (his thermos open
thick grey coffee steam rising to his lips)—

sat in the back as sirens split the night

now full of bleeding bouncers
who saw nothing in a barroom painted
with a disc jockey's smatterings

his music still pumping your heart
like a small wound cut with loathing—

colouring the homeless dead

i

a tall tree   shelters rain water
in the cold shade   where dull leaves
bend in the wind   and guard the cloud-splashed
graveyard   of the unwanted dead

crows dangling   along thick tree limbs
starlings pick at the grass and hop between paths
of those described "syphilitic" "psychotic" "schizophrenic"
"suicidal" "mad"   in a report on indigent funerals
a short   two page summary of current expenses
"$2.6 million   for 1,074 bodies (not including
burial or cremation)"   signed by the general manager
homes for the aged   an aging bureaucrat in a troubled sinecure
looking out from behind cigarette smoke   into fading
light of an office   far from the homeless damned

ii

chestnuts falling   on wet brown grass
each body lies   without memories
grieved   by freelance mourners
in the damp field   gardened to place those
no one knows   into the opened earth

no gravestones   but small square markers
hand-chiselled limestone   set in rows
across a wide rust-coloured field   with names
dates, brief epitaphs   the thin details of those
who fell into the shadows   of a tall maple tree
its gnarled trunk   choked with vine
its staunch branches   swaying in the winds

its firm limbs hanging over   the silver-frosted ground
while black smoke rises   from a nearby smokestack
into the light blue   translucent sky

iii
a cool draft   sweeping dark containers
loaded like beds   into the dull white wall
with bodies   frozen before burial
cold storage holds 100 at a time
felled   by heroin aids tuberculosis
crack   hypothermic seizures convulsing
the angry or soft-spoken   alcoholic pill-popping chain-smokers
in deep freeze   in the hope some family member can be found

on patrol in days of rain   dripping chilled
disdain   and teeth   tar-stained with indifference
a police officer   on a blue bicycle   takes out notepad
records one "found 3:23 a.m.   huddled like straw
in a wet box   full of mould   what a stench death has
been here all day   hovering like some invisible vulture
wings spread   over the helpless   kill"

iv
never any start to this   only an end
stamens break from tree limbs   brown leaves
torn by merciless winds   hit ground
as the dead   sink into shadows
with the smell   of cooking sherry   rubbing alcohol
rising from barely-parted   stiffened lips
of those   who were silent   and those
who went hungry   and those who were cold
night after night   in public places shopping malls
asleep on benches   near downtown office towers

and the dark grim walls of detention centres   where a policeman notes
"he seemed to sit and slouch   then was still
i thought he had one too many   so walked away
returned after coffee   an hour or so
he hadn't moved   i guess he just sat down and died"

v

an open casket   four hours viewing
in a barely-used corner   of a funeral parlour

eyes shut tight   forehead
powdered smooth   as if light-toned ceramic
fired and cooled   the body now motionless
lying   in a particle-board
box reserved for city-paid burials
where only two graveyards
accept the freight   (holy cross and beechwood)
and where the abandoned   sight is marked
without flowers or prayers   without
family   recounting favoured memories
without   a lifelong companion to sing
the right of passage   thru the impenetrable dark—

only with leaves   falling
in this severed   space

the beginnings   of ignorance and sight—

drums and piano

for cecil taylor and andrew cyrille

diaspora

she
spent her days
in an office, thinking
about a world full of
drums, flutes, bonfires
autumn harvests
when the villagers
dressed their men
in paint and bird
feathers, the women
wore robes handwoven,
embroidered
with symbols of fertility, fat
snakes and fish and
horns of plenty, all aglow
the bright threads
of celebration, what became
the substance of dance,
the pearls of laughter,
bodies coupling, wet
with sweat and palm oil,
upon a patch of earth,
a sacred place of offering
nearby the camp where the flesh
of puberty each year
was shorn, left to appease
ancestors, the spirits
of coming generations
she dreamed over
a cup of coffee, in a
room amidst others who were

unable to hear
the shriek of jungle
birds, the cries
of lovers beneath the
palm fronds of dawn, or words
festering like sores
on her mouth,
helping to build
out of skulls and old
bones, a throne of anger,
burst of sudden
laughter, or any other
purposeful detour
from weeping

paradox

for charlie parker and martin luther king, jr.

in the final moment   it's what we learn from the body
how it is seen   atop a sterile chrome table
covered in white cloth   the blood
now stuck   in the breath—

whether the mouth   was a sax or microphone
it wore out   all their stress

and became   an addiction
with the openness   of moonlight
pushing in   on their dark brown foreheads—

it was then   they were held
to god truth   and white powder
their full weight   lying inert

some doctor poked each   with a tube
said   "looks like

someone   in his sixties"
even tho   they both beat this by more than twenty years—

this is what it ate of them   the hate and bitterness
envy and long solitudes   a penetrating sight

showed in their lungs   scarred tissue
along the heart's wall   gave
sign   they had lived

beyond the time   any might suspect
from their birth   certificates—

34 and 39   and what remains to tell in their absence—

they each defined   what the world could only show them
violence   at first instance

stinging   like sorrow
their nostrils   clogged with pain—

free jazz

there's a hollowness in the evening few understand
it's the sound of trumpets and piss in the hallways

the screeching bass and an elevator crowded with smoke
the piano keys banging stairwells' blinking lights

the violin scratching amidst gunfire
a guitar screaming from a car's back seat

how can anyone explain the drums?
what words make sense of the wild saxophone?

if you don't know this world you won't want to enter it
it's not one of those walks where you don't mind getting lost

coming home late may not be an option
coming home tomorrow may not happen at all

the yellow dahlias' blossoms cannot guide you this
night sharp winds will only drown out your cries

on streets where the unspeakable has its torment
because it knows nobody is listening and even less care

these are the homes out of which musicians leap
and you refuse to hear them because it will shatter your ears

then you would know for the first time the trauma of your longing
the painted walkways that open like arteries into a lifeless sea

our turn

for the former premier of ontario and his comments on "black-focused schools"

"Only a fool would let their enemy educate their children."
—MALCOLM X

we start "our" month this way   february
unrelenting snow   only now do we get "our history"

even tho we are told   we must take our lessons
in some one else's rooms   and hold ourselves in silence

ignore all that came before   ships unloaded weapons
and great empires fell into wars   bartering many

into masts and compass   winds worked west
toward an ever-widening   horizon

where several swallowed seas
or were struck by a fire   they had never before seen—

and this   stayed over centuries
as if fixed in the claws   of disfigured demons

their wings melting into the smoke   we breathe
our words   float out like torn sails

we keep what we've carried inside our wounds

there is no mocking anything   then
our masks   and dances

left in an old tree   by a deep river
of memory   and fear

on toronto streets

she marched up steps
the same march

she had seen so many times
as a child

when photos on newspapers
transported her into a land of cities

where she saw sidewalks bleached pebbled
street corners bright lights and stop signs—

some called this paradise
cold and wet in winter

despotic and damp in summer—
yet she longed for this like a vesper

to shatter whatever stood in her way—

borders chalk marking dark bodies
splashed against grey—

and still she walked right into it
eyes full of contradictions

between what she thought would be
bar lights dance floors late-night restaurants

but what instead was at her door each day
she found the most suffering

a life in her hands drying petals of an early crocus
as she leaned over twilight at the edge of a ravine

a woodpecker hammering the breeze

doorway of no return

> "it's an unspeakable anger i have...there was just so much evil. i don't think i am in a position to forgive. i am not fine. i am not fine at all. i don't know if i'll ever be fine again."
>
> —NICOLE JAMES, of yensomu youth and development project who travelled to ghana with others to mark the 200-year anniversary of the end of the slave trade

and it was certainly a journey
across time into circumstance
across oceans that sucked up villagers

who walked with sunlight on ghana's shores
and crawled into castles over parched sands
that ground down bones and blood

over steps that sponged spit and shit
and rooms where pregnant women had their bellies split
and cells where hot irons stenciled backs and chests

past corridors where bowels fed the earth
past walls where a thousand or more
were crushed into each other like foul meat

where men and women without water
drank sweat off each others' foreheads

where soldiers came every night
for "belly warmers" who in nine months bore light-skinned servants

into spaces where the rebellious met their death
and down narrow black walkways where the ocean roared
and only the blind could see into seemingly endless waters

where blue-black bodies at dawn were led
with chains on fishing boats to large ships
full of foul men rifles and whips

shouting orders or cutting the breath
of any who would not or could not move along—

these were what were marked like parcels
owned by someone somewhere far away
across an ocean diseased with ships

property recorded beneath stacked decks
bringing them into fields houses farmyards and sheds
or plotting all night to discharge into moonlit waves
or make ships return to shores they were led from
so they might find once again the winds of the earth

they knew by birth and to which they would never return
neither here nor in a moment of mercy until centuries
have gone under sails and their bones pebble the earth

and their children roam forgetful
of who they were and how and why they arrived
and those who came before and had no names

and could not claim what they made in
towns and cities where they were always set aside
until some young men and women journeyed

far beyond what space and time
could ever reveal—

dominion

they know what they have by what they carry—
bank cards silk ties cufflinks battle scars
and islands where stones shine like light—

they forget the slaughter and those
who chose to go under at that moment
when that green wall kept others down

they watched the ocean open
and the songs sucked up within
the current of centuries that rose
with the swell of bodies
that could never return—

so we live without their stories
unless we find them in some spirit world
begging the authentic in an apartment
above a fruit store disguised in the words
of a smiling rasta summoning rain clouds
in the suddenness of day—

in this moment of unusual glory
there are so many things thrown into despair
like a noose in the hands of white boys
hanging around trees at a high school

or outside an ivy league professor's door
or on the cover of golf week magazine
and in the mail of black corrections officers
threatening their lives—

they never wonder what's common
in this every day extraordinary made ordinary
by repetition nothing is original

especially the harm that passes for wisdom
injected like serum their lewd gestures
dragging the disobedient to their knees

as if what they cannot control will not exist
and you can speak only in echo

and they provide the words—

mumia

and so we read the protests
of his announced death
the words like rusted daggers

each syllable speaking so many centuries
when we relied on hope when weapons were unavailable
we sought deliverance in the heart of snails—

what was discovered was undeniable
we wrapped our wounds in tissue paper
to keep blood from flooding our arms—

nothing seemed given in return
we got what we took the raw wraps of heaven
rainbows floating into an exuberance rarely seen—

what flew over us on this flight on this ocean
salted with bodies the sick suicidal mad
we felt their breaths like aches in our bones—

so many handed down after so many centuries
what it must have been like not being able to swim
in a vast relentless deep and cold ocean

or spattered bone and blood
between leg and wrist irons
long after we let go our bowels
in the bottom of a boat
destined to death or a new world—

and now
another 500 years later
another black man they want to die—

in a time when they say all are equal
we are caught in this moment

like smoke in distant trees—

pas de deux

passing things   a theatre of hands
gathering pansies morning glories sweet pea to place into a vase
bells from the balcony   night winds making window box petals ring
so clear   she could see into veils of ecstasy
out of the window screen   a dust rag now in her left hand
her coffee cool as a breath   in the other hand
moving slow to mouth   sorrowful as dull brown eyes
over small rooms   full of lovers children dust
while fire engine ambulance police car   siren bleak day
with a shrill blaring   she could not call loveliness or horror
the noises routine as tasks   soft kisses on her cheek
the pale alarms pink dawn   after deep blue twilight sex

this consistency she determined by her tongue   its
soft red meat reference for quality   all that she could taste
each drop of rain   falling from july the glittering sky
where sometimes she saw angels   watering gardens of cloud
their wings   hot sheets of diamond
burning holes   in the vast space of reason
he said to her *"i love you"*   then took a train ride
into the hollows of another city   hid where he could
dark hallways   the wine closets of her memory
where she recalls finding her father sprawled out   toothless
a sack of clothing   worn colours smelling yellow piss

*

still   she would think of him
and others   in a dim-lit room
with pea green curtains   a crucifix
shadowing the bed

two candles   burning
above the warmth of bodies
in a tight   measure for measure
she gasps sighs   slowly
from beneath   her legs
parting wings of a black swan
while music played   softly
she could hear   blues
the heart   in tendrils
plucked guitar   strings
strumming for years and years
'til spring becomes   longing
a cool stream   racing to the lips
she sings   it is the same song
billie bessie ma rainey knew

"my man he don't love me,
he treat me awful mean.
i say my man he don't love me,
he treat me awful mean."

her eyes sharp as cut glass   a yearning
perched to windows   the children asleep in their rooms
she would watch   the back
of one man the back of others
sweat slithering
down dark spines   something groaning
her belly once again   she thought
it had to do with
"the pig foot   gut stew
stinking diapers of shit
weeks of laundry   never done
then cheque day"   he would return
she made each room   fresh as a bower
with cut flowers   dusted tabletops couch chairs

for that man who comes home
a new face new song new strings
on his guitar he plays the backwater blues
she sings

"my man he don't love me,
he treat me awful mean."

*

what worries her most is the torment
of thought the sudden anxiety of each
nerve cell responding to loneliness
like a caged thing hungry for meat
she whimpers growls over the empty
watering cans picks up fallen petals
bread crumbs pieces of paper from the table
wipes sleep from her eyes her hands
a cruelness while yellow flowers grow
young birds into wings ready
as falcons to discover trails to heaven
where sometimes she imagines her mother
driven by a chauffeur who wears white
tie tails thin black ellington mustache
the staccato of a barrel house piano a playful
melody beyond a tall silver gate that opens
to the laughter of a rent party the landlord
is too afraid to enter

but this is a joy she cannot keep her
mind an iron steaming with all the things
beyond her reach what she sees
on the other side of windows furs jewelry
perfume patent shoes a hand to find the warmth
of her hand day after day

the same hand   sure as a consequence
she knows she will not have so she collects
herself from the worn couch   bids her
daydreams be sensible   calls other emotions
from the night the falling rain the cold
districts of her heart   city streets
where her lovers laugh   and think
of bedrooms breakfasts   nothing down
no key needed   and no responsibility

*

sometimes
it can be this way
otherwise
in the onslaught
of night
as if to protect
herself
she reaches into silence
memory
her glass of musings
like a cat ready to sleep
while clear water moves
a warm stillness in the bath
she slowly sinks
into bright light
the shining reflection
her face finally relaxed
she succumbs to the artistry
of routine and recalls her body
responding like a charged particle
to the physics of need
the dull white powder room smelling of cheap perfume
the no-frills shopping carts full of bags of bread

the stove coils red as veins wound into bursting
the vacuum push-broom clearing pathways in each room
the dark hands cracked as old plates
without realizing their fullness
or the slow rise of perspiration
on her face concealing
edges of emotions that crawl
like insects into her heart
as she wipes soap from her flesh
then watches the water become
grey memory

*

other days   flustered and lost she slides
into anguish like an eel   as her hopes become an inconvenience
and the years turn to water in her hands   cold as a lake
filtered thru her fingers in the third month of a long darkness
when the sun falls like a coin   behind the hills of winter
and she can see shadows   lunge like chased squirrels
into thin twigs shrubbery   the root of which
will never be discovered until it become an archeologist's prize
centuries after she lay down before the guardian of endless sleep

but for now   she reads into her palm of days
sees the lines that form and crack   sees the once sharp black
turn lusterless grey   sees the firm fixed fingers
inherit trembling   the fingernail polish chipped away
as her children grow   their mouths waking into anger
while she speaks in solitude   and her words
return to her   she talks daylong into mirrors
does not interpret herself   is often misquoted
the mirror like a soldier   speaking for itself
with a deep voice   the words of a man
tell her   she is like a broken music box
with a dancer   smelling of frankincense and oil
or other fragrances that will prepare her   for a parade of kings

hoodoo inna diffa-rent style

"i had to meet the white man's eyes. an unfamiliar weight burdened me . . . i was battered down by tom-toms, cannabilism, intellectual deficiency, racial defects . . ."
—F. FANON, from *Black Skin, White Masks*

"caught them slitting the throats
of chickens above grave sites
in the lurid half-light
of a winter
2:17 a.m.
white candles dripping
wax upon white snow
and voices mumbling gibberish
to a far-off god
who slept in a land
of palm trees and revolution
with a people intent upon a slaughter
for so simple a thing as freedom
only to wake and discover
the passage of the dead
into something less recognizable
than confusion and misery
or the low trumpet moans
of rituals told and re-told
by some aspiring blind man
as if he were a reminder
that there are songs
the living sing
in their ignorance
and the dead hear
with ears full of sorrow
for what they did not know
when they had the chance

to stand beside gravestones
with quarrelling chickens
while the red lights of police squad cars
made the trail of blood seem
a mile long"

"5 jolts, 17 minutes needed to execute indiana murderer"

"the symbols of social order—the police, the bugle calls in the barracks, military parades and the waving flags,—are at one and the same time inhibitory and stimulating: for they do not convey the message 'don't dare to budge'; rather, they cry out 'get ready to attack'".

—F. FANON, from *Black Skins, White Masks*

is a headline that has eyes
black against white
newsprint popping up
from the lap of someone who sits
next to me on a streetcar
and i wonder what it must be like
to sit for all that time
next to no-one
hands and legs
strapped to a chair of electricity
prisoner of a game
wild and unyielding
the body like a drill
spinning thru charged air
and contorted to the agony
of that which makes things
equal and common
ignores race sex other distinctions
and looks only at the thing
that makes night skies
jump with excitement
a jagged edge of fire
breathing out of heaven
and illuminating the thing
as it was before conception

a simple molecular structure
ashes to ashes dust to dust
the fossil of matter
or persons close by
prisoners of dread that
a morning newspaper looks back
with the eyes of the dead—

guesswork

"why not quite the simple attempt to touch the other,
to feel the other, to explain the other to myself?"
—F. FANON, from *Black Skins, White Masks*

sometimes the blue
happens this way all over
without specific request
just that large eye opening
unblemished rising yellow
so that things might be clearly
seen without a microscope
as the shuttle of sudden events
blazes into a view of history
wherein everything is
decipherable as code
and you see the blackness
of bodies caught up in a pit
hard bones pressed
against the tightening of skin
teeth trapped in the halfway
of soft gums and sleepless pain
arms legs fingers feet
feeble as a newborn
senseless as if anesthetized
held to a grudging
spot in a corner
of hope and imperishable goodness
or whatever the conditions
are that flower into love
and the nearness of bodies
lost in so simple an ecstasy
that the earth must stop and acknowledge

there is something that creates this
but it is not here at the moment
and the view is not original
just the common occurrence of horror
just thin wings beating on
the back of a fearsome apparition
just clouds hanging black
making ready an ambush on sunrise
and the flesh of someone you
know is turning over
the white flames of a spit
on a wind-littered white beach
where the ocean is an endless
rage—

a poem for anytime like now

"they are after themselves. they call it destiny. progress. we call it 'haints'. haints of their victims rising from the sun of africa, south america, asia."

—I. REED, from *Mumbo Jumbo*

wind over waters
like a hand touching a face
the city an old sore
upon the heavy earth
skies so blue they create
an infinity
separate from any existence
a sock from a shoe
only in the imagination
whose pearls are a sequel
of longing
that is not yours
nor mine
but belongs to the particular person
caught at the particular moment
in the particular act
perhaps he will be black
or the he will be a she
and she will be black
and they will hire her to kill
one boulder with two stats-can
ceic unemployment classifications
they can pay less than minimum wage
it will not be some job in a sweat shop
god has long since learned the tricks
of technology operates state of the art
apple II computers some scientific

adam invented
werner von braun in the labs
of fritz lang's metropolis
berlin or cape kennedy what difference
he is not a jew
nor are his creations
he has built a pandemonium
on top of milton's
pandemonium
they call it space shuttle explorations star wars
they call it civilization progress democracy move over
they are hurtling from darkness into darkness
no this time it is not africa
chile india china vietnam
this time it is not gas chambers ovens
sharecropper shacks apartheid lynch mobs
this time they call it escape get away let's beat it
the village is burning the goddamn black plague they mean
black people
they have been running from since the middle ages
they call it barbarians always on the borders
they call it polite names and wish it would sleep
but the waters rise up in flame with the winds
a torch for a hand a slap in the face
earth sore an old infringement
heavy upon the city
so romulus killed remus built rome and cursed
his children
made tar babies of them all
who later told stories
of what happens when you are reared
by wolves—

resisting slaughter

i give you a string of morning glories
on a dark and wet spring sunday

where even the birds are quiet
and buds of trees outside my window

hold their growth for a moment as if to breathe
the soundless beauty of their return—

somewhere a mother holds a child who is dying
her arms full of a young body exuding last breaths

chest stiffening like a plank of seed
eyes fixed on a withering sea breeze

where young men wait with weapons in deep trenches
for words that will make them abandon their hearts—

somewhere else women and men pull pails
of water filled with waste and floating fish

from a river sitting at the fount of a factory
controlled by a person in another country

bleached substances spilling out of an underground
circuit of tubes connected to vats of disease—

time implodes here in a cavity of space
and light melts into an indecipherable dark

and all things are without air
and gravity loosens like a mist

particles spanning over the earth in a moment
the sun dislodged from its orbit like a roman fireball—

i turn to you then with an offering simple as sunrise
inimitable and translucent as mist over mountains

as the cry of a loon on an abandoned lake
as a bear waking hungry from a winter cave

as stars peeking into just-born galaxies
flaring like the white hot metal of a blacksmith's hands—

Acknowledgements

The author wishes to acknowledge grants he has received from the Ontario Arts Council Writers' Reserve Program and the Toronto Arts Council Writers' Grants Program for this work.

Some poems in this collection have appeared previously in the following publications:

Anti-Racism in Education: Missing in Action (Canadian Centre for Policy Alternatives); *The Great Black North* (Frontenac House Poetry); *Fleurette Africaine* (wind in the leaves collective); *Prairie Fire;* and *Canadian Ethnic Studies.*